REAL

I Know How I Feel™

Sophia Day®

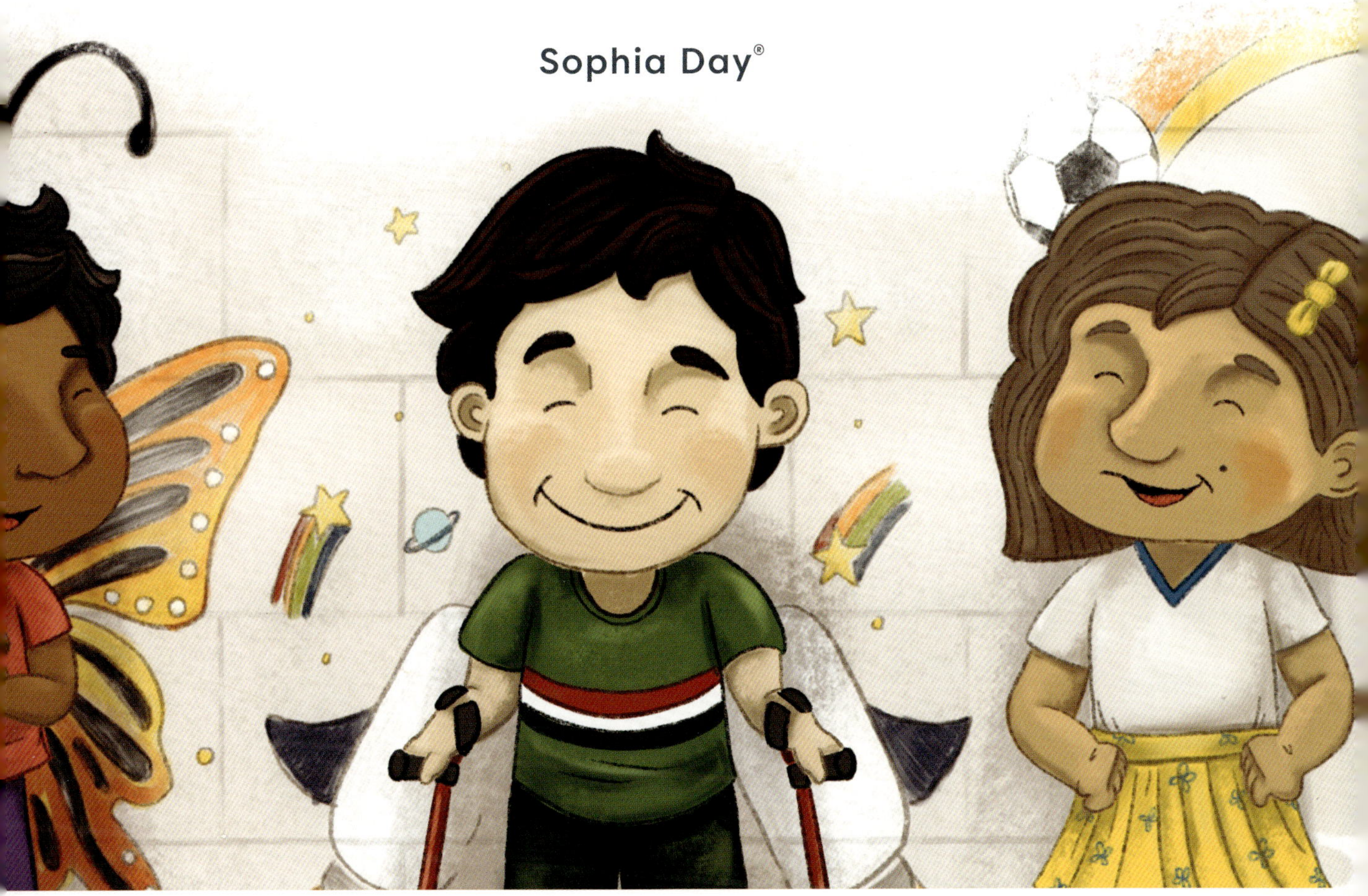

Written by Megan Johnson   Illustrated by Stephanie Strouse

The Sophia Day® Creative Team-
Megan Johnson, Stephanie Strouse,
Kayla Pearson, Timothy Zowada, Celestte Dills, Mel Sauder

A **special thank you** to our team of reviewers who graciously give us feedback, edits, and help ensure that our products remain accurate, applicable, and genuinely diverse.

Text and pictures copyrighted © 2020 by MVP Kids Media, LLC.

All rights reserved. No part of this publication may be reproduced in whole or in part by any mechanical, photographic, or electronic process, or in the form of any audio or video recording, nor may it be stored in a retrieval system or transmitted in any form or by any means now known or hereafter invented or otherwise copied for public or private use without the written permission of MVP Kids Media, LLC.

Published and Distributed by MVP Kids Media, LLC -
Mesa, Arizona, USA
Printed by Prosperous Printing Inc. -
Shenzhen, China

Designed by Stephanie Strouse

ISBN 9781645169703
DOM May 2020
Job #11-009-01

When my day is a wreck
and my sister won't share,
my favorite toy broke
and life doesn't seem fair—

I say that I'm sorry. Mom fixes my toy, and I think of a game that we all can enjoy.

I feel *peaceful*.

Tell about a time you felt peaceful.

When Grandma goes bye-bye
or I've lost my stuffed bear,
when my friends can't come play
or it seems no one cares—

my body moves slowly.

I can't help but cry.

I need someone to hold me

and wipe tears from my eyes.

I feel sad.

What makes you feel better when you feel sad?

But I look for the good,
and I find treasures lost.
I wake up from sweet dreams
snuggling somebody soft.

Things are going my way,

at least for a while.

I share my good feelings

and make someone smile.

I feel **happy**.

How can you make someone else feel happy?

It's my first day at school,

and there's no one I know.

Nobody says "hi,"

so I play all alone.

I feel like they're staring.

Oh, what do they think?

Am I odd? Or invisible?

Maybe I stink?

I feel *lonely*.

What is it like to feel lonely?

My teacher is kind, and she helps me make friends. They stay by my side until the day ends.

We play all day long until time to dismiss. Then, my dad picks me up with a hug and a kiss!

I feel *loved*.

When do you feel loved? How can you help others feel loved?

When it's my turn to talk,

    I don't know what to say.

I look down at my toes,

    wish I could hide away.

Everyone's watching,
and I wish I could shrink.
I feel weak. My legs shake,
and my face blushes pink.

I feel *shy*.

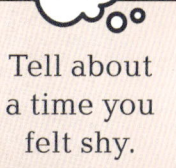

Tell about a time you felt shy.

When I meet a new friend,

I say, "Hi, what's your name?"

"Do you want to be friends?"

or "Let's go play a game!"

I smile and offer to share my supplies.
I ask for a hug and give lots of high fives!

I feel **friendly**.

How did you make a new friend recently?

Today it's my turn
to show and to tell.
My tummy feels sick,
and I didn't sleep well.

When I'm in the spotlight, all eyes are on me. Will I make a mistake that everyone sees?

I feel *nervous*.

When do you feel nervous?

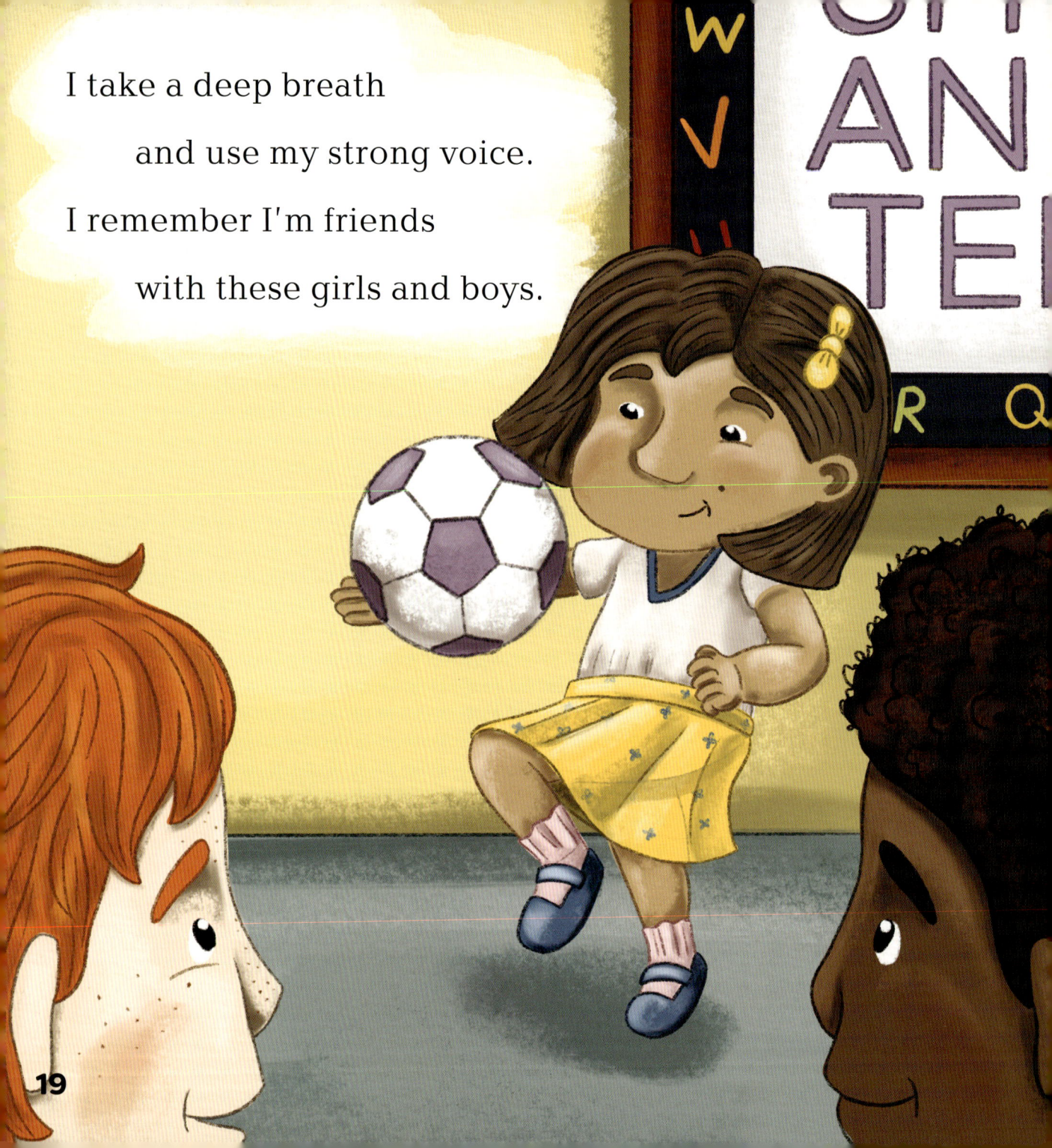

I take a deep breath
 and use my strong voice.
I remember I'm friends
 with these girls and boys.

And if things don't work out
just according to plan,
I'll learn from mistakes
'cause I know that I can!

I feel *brave*.

When do you feel the most brave?

When I think I'm alone or I've had a bad dream, my heart beats too fast, and I can't seem to breathe.

When I see a stranger
or try something new,
when it's dark or I'm lost
and don't know what to do—

I feel scared.

When do you feel scared?

So I hold Baba's hand,
and we turn on a light.
I run to my mama,
and she holds me tight.

I always stay near them wherever we go. I take some deep breaths, and my heart starts to slow.

I feel safe.

Where do you feel the most safe?

Some days, there are times I don't know how I feel. My mind spins around like a big Ferris wheel.

I don't know what I want
or what I need now.
I laugh and I cry
all together somehow.

I feel confused.

When have you felt both happy and sad at the same time?

I'm happy about
  all the things I can do,
and I feel really big
  when I learn something new!

I feel
confident.

What is something you do well?

Learn feelings with our mvpkids.

Lucas Miller

I feel angry.

I feel peaceful.

LeBron Miller

I feel sad.

I feel happy.

Yong Chen

I feel lonely.

I feel loved.

Aanya Patel

I feel shy.

I feel friendly.

Julia Rojas

I feel nervous.

I feel brave.

Miriam Nasser

I feel scared.

I feel safe.

Leo Russo

I feel confused.

I feel confident.

Also featuring: Gabby González

HELPFUL TEACHING TIPS
Head. Heart. Hand.

Informing Minds

Emotional Intelligence—defined as one's acceptance of self, ability to regulate one's emotions, and understanding another person's point of view—is a more reliable indicator of happiness and success in life than one's IQ. Although children are born with a natural temperament, the way parents and caregivers interact with them will affect their emotional intelligence.

People with stable emotional health are shown to have better physical health. The way your child consistently resolves his or her own feelings wires the brain through chemical reactions. If a child's emotional coping skills are positive, his or her body chemistry will reflect these positive hormones. An overload of stress hormones affects physical health and emotional well-being.

Moving Hearts

Parents who give positive and predictable attention to their children help the children learn to manage their behavior and their emotions. Being fully present with your children will help them feel safe and confident to share their emotions.

It is natural for children to wonder whether their difficult emotions make them a bad person. Be sure to accept emotions ("It's okay to feel angry that she took your toy...") before addressing a behavior ("...but because you threw the car, you need to sit with me until you're acting safely."). Praise your child when he or she manages a strong feeling without a challenging behavior.

Calmly narrate your own emotional situations so that your children can have a window into your feelings and how you handle them. They will begin to manage feelings the same way they see you doing so. When children see that big feelings can be expressed calmly, they will feel more comfortable with talking about and handling emotions.

When you teach coping skills such as breathing or visualization exercises, remember to introduce the activity when your child is calm, not in the middle of an emotional outburst. Consistent practice during calm times will help your child's brain and body access the coping skill during times of distress.

Use picture books or flash cards to help your child identify emotions and develop empathy. Have your child point out what features they see on someone's face when they feel happy, sad, or angry. Draw a set of faces on index cards, or make your own set of emotions pictures with your child expressing different feelings.

Sign language can significantly help children who have a hard time verbally communicating their feelings. Start by teaching one or two signs at a time, and use them consistently, making the sign and saying the word together. Remember that children need a lot of repetition before they will use the sign on their own.

Discuss synonyms for emotion words and talk about the nuances in similar words such as mad, frustrated, angry, and annoyed, or happy, joyful, excited, and proud. The more emotional words children have in their vocabulary, the more clearly they will be able to express themselves and have empathy for others.

Directing Hands

*For additional tip and reference information, visit **www.mvpkids.com**.*

Our **CELEBRATE!™** board books for toddlers and preschoolers focus on social, emotional, educational, and physical needs. Helpful Teaching Tips are included in each book to equip parents to guide their children deeper into the subject of each book.

Our **Playful Apprentice™** for ages 4-8 pairs factual text with imaginative illustrations. Readers are invited to roleplay a variety of community roles and career options. Each book includes interviews and advice from real-life professionals.

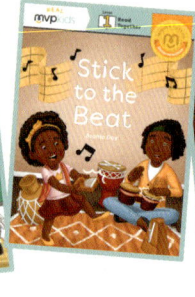
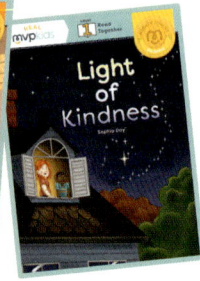

Our **Mighty Tokens™** paperback series helps emerging readers learn positive concepts with an experienced reader. Parents or mentors read one side of the page and children read the other side. Each book deposits tokens of affirmation into children so that they may someday become mighty adults.

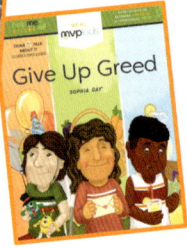

Our **Help Me Become™** series for early elementary readers tells three short stories of our MVP Kids® inspiring character growth. Each story concludes with a discussion guide to help your child process the story and apply the concepts.

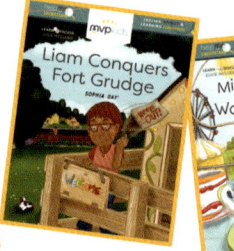
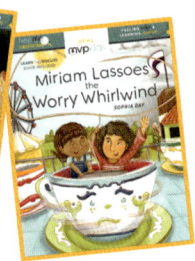

Our **Help Me Understand™** series for elementary readers shares the stories of our MVP Kids® learning to understand and manage a specific emotion. Readers will gain tools to take responsibility for their own emotions and and develop healthy coping skills.

Ages 4-8

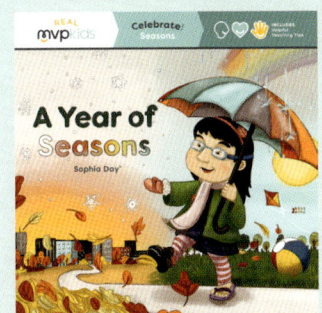
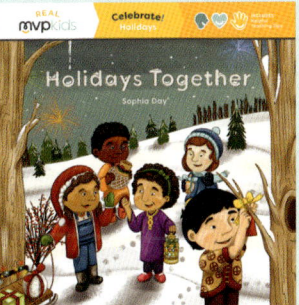
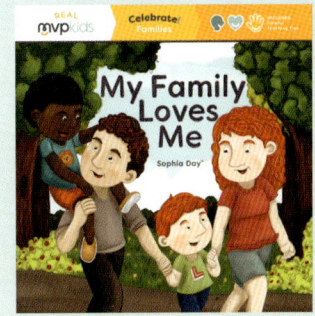

Our **Celebrate!**™ paperback books for Pre-K to Grade 2 focus on social and emotional learning. Helpful Teaching Tips are included to equip mentors and parents. These books are perfect for classrooms and home schooling!

We have apps!

Our interactive e-book apps are designed to expand the experience of our content. Functions include audio of Sophia Day® reading the book, learn-to-read options, and interactive games.

Available on Apple and Google Play App Stores, use keyword "MVP Kids."

SOPHIA DAY'S® instill™

Social Emotional Learning (SEL) Program for Early Learners
- *Entire year's worth of SEL lesson plans*
- *8 MVP Kids® puppets*
- *Audio tracks and many more resources to build a classroom full of MVP Kids®!*
- *Find more information at www.mvpkidsED.com*

WWW.MVPKIDS.COM